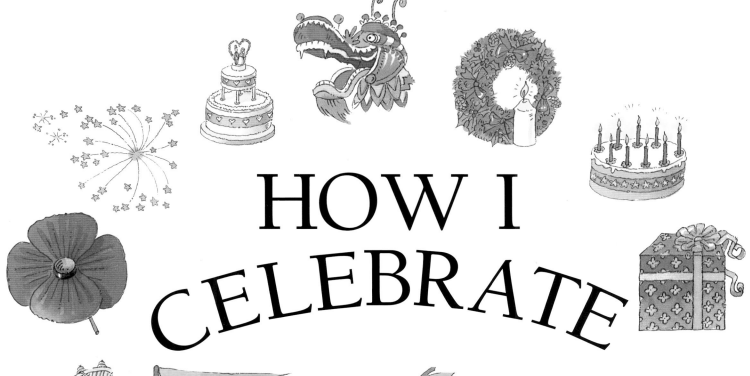

HOW I CELEBRATE

Pam Robson

TRANSEDITION

Published in 2001 by Transedition Ltd.

This edition printed for Chapters in Spain.
Artes Gráficas Toledo S.A.U.
D.L. TO: 1757-2000

ISBN 1 898250 76 6

10 9 8 7 6 5 4 3 2 1

Credits
How I Celebrate was produced for Transedition
Limited by Bender Richardson White, Uxbridge.

Project Manager: Lionel Bender
Designer and Art Editor: Ben White
Text Editor: Clare Oliver
US Text Editor: Dandi Mackall
Make-up: Michael Weintroub, MW Graphics
Picture Research: Cathy Stastny & Lionel Bender

Main Artwork: Teri Gower and Pamela Hewetson
  Historical Artwork: Mark Bergin
Studio Photography: Steve Gorton

Religious symbols and items provided by
Articles of Faith, Bury, BL9 6BU (telephone:
  0161 763 6232) – thanks to Christine Howard
Publishing Director: Edward Glover
Production: Richard Johnson
Cover Design: Mike Pilley, Pelican Graphics

Consultants:
Martin E. Marty – Fairfax M. Cone Distinguished
  Service Professor Emeritus of the History of
  Modern Christianity, The University of
  Chicago, USA; Director of the Public
  Religion Project.
Alan Brown, The National Society (Church of
  England) for Promoting Religious Education.

Contents

Different Celebrations

There are many ways to celebrate. It can be enjoying yourself on a special occasion. It can be honoring a person's life, or a great event that has made the world a better place. It can also be performing a special religious ceremony. Every day, someone somewhere is celebrating. A celebration is a happy event, when people come together. Religious celebrations are often holidays, when people do not have to go to school or work. They are times of prayer, worship, and remembrance.

Grace

My name is Grace. I am an American. I live in Memphis. My religion is Baptist, a part of Christianity. My ancestors came from Africa. My favorite celebration is New Year's Eve. My family, friends, and I have a party at home and at midnight we sing *Auld Lang Syne*.

Hideo

My name is Hideo. I am nine years old. I live in Japan. I look forward to Kodomo-no-hi. It is a special day for Japanese boys. My little sister looks forward to Hina Matsuri, the special day for Japanese girls. She likes to wear her *kimono*.

Yasmin

I am Yasmin. My family comes from Saudi Arabia in the Middle East. I have a baby brother. When he was born, my father whispered words to him from our holy book, the *Qur'an*. When my brother is bigger, I will tell him about my favorite celebration, Id-ul-Fitr.

Lionel

I am Lionel. I live in New York City, but some of my relatives live in Israel. We are Jewish. Every Saturday we attend synagogue. Saturday is our Sabbath, a rest day. I look forward to being 13 years old. Then it will be time for my Bar Mitzvah. Afterwards I will be treated like a grown-up.

Not all celebrations are religious ones. They can be small family occasions, friendly local celebrations, or even international events. They can be about old traditions and customs. Some involve dancing and being noisy; others are a time for quiet thoughts. Celebrations may take place in homes, in places of worship, or outdoors.

Bernadette

I am Bernadette. I live in France. I am nearly nine years old. I am a Roman Catholic, a part of the Christian religion. I am looking forward to my First Communion. I have a new white dress to wear. I have two birthdays, because I also have a name day on St. Bernadette's Day.

Gita

My name is Gita. I live in England, but my family comes from India. We are Hindus. Hindu ceremonies are called *samsaras*. A person's wedding is called the 13th *samsara*. I look forward to my sister's wedding. She will wear a red and gold *sari*.

Sven

I am Sven. I live in Sweden where the winters are cold and dark. I am a Christian. I belong to the Lutheran Church. My favorite celebration is Christmas. We decorate our homes, and everyone exchanges cards and presents.

Different Calendars

Most people use the Gregorian calendar, which dates from the birth of Jesus Christ. The letters BC (Before Christ) refer to years before his birth. The letters AD (*Anno Domini*, Latin for "year of our Lord") refer to years after it. The Gregorian, or "everyday," calendar has 12 months, from January to December. It is a solar calendar, which means it is based on the movements of the Earth around the Sun.

A lunar month is based on the time it takes for the Moon to pass through its main stages: new Moon, first quarter, full Moon, and last quarter.

Lunar Calendars

Each religion measures time differently. Hindus and Muslims use the lunar calendar. A lunar month is the time the Moon takes to circle the Earth—29.5 days. Each year the Muslim festival of Ramadan happens at a different time in the everyday calendar. The Jewish calendar is based on the movements of the Sun and the Moon, so Jewish Yom Kippur may be celebrated in September or October.

Christian children make special sweet foods for Christmas.

Preparing to Celebrate

We look at the calendar for the dates of celebrations. Preparing for a celebration is great fun. We may shop for gifts and cards, or make decorations. We may want to prepare special foods. Hindus make delicious sweets for Divali. People bake mince pies for Christmas, and birthday parties always need a birthday cake. In Japan and China, sticky rice cakes are a traditional treat.

Family Celebrations

As well as official dates marked on calendars as holidays and feast days, there are special family celebrations, such as birthdays, anniversaries, or graduation days. Everyone looks forward to celebrating their own birthday, as well as the birthdays of friends and relatives. Wedding anniversaries are celebrated each year by married couples. After 25 years, couples celebrate their silver wedding anniversary and, after 50 years, they celebrate their golden wedding.

Couples celebrate their ruby wedding anniversary after 40 years of marriage.

Harvest Festivals

Time can be measured by the passing of the seasons. In the north and south, there are four seasons—spring, summer, fall, and winter. Farmers rely on the Sun to ripen their crops, which is why the solar calendar developed. In the fall, people give thanks for the harvest of fruit, by holding special harvest festivals.

People on the tropical island of Bali, in southeast Asia, celebrate their harvest by carrying pyramids of fruit and flowers to their local shrine. These will be offered to the gods, in thanks for the harvest.

Holidays

The USA has ten official holidays:
1. **New Year's Day**
2. **Martin Luther King, Jr., Day**
3. **Presidents' Day**
4. **Memorial Day**
5. **Independence Day**
6. **Labor Day**
7. **Columbus Day**
8. **Veterans' Day**
9. **Thanksgiving**
10. **Christmas**

Keeping a Diary

Writing a daily diary is a way to make a calendar of your life. When you are older you can look back and remember all the fun you had. Happy times become happy memories, if you write them down.

Many people write their diary in the evening, when the events of the day are fresh in their minds.

7

One Big Family

People of different religions and cultures live close together in cities all over the world. All of them have their own customs and traditions. But everyone, including those with no religious beliefs, can join in during traditional celebrations.

Confusing Names

Reading about different celebrations can be confusing because some of their names have several different spellings or words. For example, Thai Buddhists celebrate Vaisakha, which Sri Lankan Buddhists call Wesak. Other spelling or word variations include:

Dassehra, Dassera, or Dusshera

Divali or Diwali

Eid-ul-Fitr or Id-ul-Fitr

Asalha Perahera, Esala Perahera, or Kandy Perahara

Shrove Tuesday or Mardi Gras

Succot, Succoth, or Sukkot

Sharing the Celebration

Living together as good neighbors, people respect each other's customs. There are many differences in the ways that people celebrate, but there are many similarities, too. As people learn more about each other, these similarities become obvious.

All over the world, exchanging gifts and cards symbolizes unity. Sharing food at feast times symbolizes togetherness and equality. Certain foods have their own symbolism. Rice is recognized in many cultures as a symbol of fertility.

Hindu children often take special Divali sweets into school, to share with their friends. Divali is the Hindu festival of lights, which takes place each winter.

8

Decorations

All over the world, symbolic objects and lucky charms are used in celebrations. British brides once carried lucky silver horseshoes at their weddings. Orange blossom was popular in bridal bouquets because it was a sign of fertility. Some jewelry traditionally brings good luck. Chinese amulets and beads carved from peach stones are believed to give protection from evil. Chinese babies wear small bells or coins on red thread to ward off bad spirits. Hindu girls give special bracelets to their brothers to wear.

Beads have a special symbolism for the Masai people of Kenya and the Ndebele people of South Africa.

Clothes

Some celebrations need special clothes. At Sikh, Hindu, and Muslim weddings, brides wear red and gold. Red is a lucky color, especially in China. Christian and Jewish brides often wear white, a sign of purity. In South Africa, Ndebele brides cover their wedding robes with white beads. But in India and China, white is worn at funerals.

Things in Common

Festivals of light are held in almost every religion because lights and fires are recognized symbols of hope, lighting the way to the future. Most people in Western Europe now send Christmas cards, whether or not they are Christian. And friends and neighbors of all faiths are invited to Hindu Divali parties. People everywhere take part in shared celebrations. Old traditions are ending and new ones are beginning.

Many different items are associated with celebrations. Special cups, symbols, and figures of gods are used in religious celebrations. Candles, greeting cards, musical instruments are used in all kinds of events.

Celebrations are special. People mark the occasion by wearing special clothes.

Birth Celebrations

Every year, 78 million babies are born and their journey of life begins. Hindus see this journey as a never-ending cycle of stages, called *samsaras*; others view life as a single path with a goal. Key stages of the journey of life are marked by celebrations.

Ibrahim's Covenant with Allah

Allah, as Muslims call God, asked Ibrahim to kill his son as a sacrifice. This was to test Ibrahim's faith. Ibrahim agreed, but Allah spared the boy. He knew that Ibrahim was faithful. Muslims regard Ibrahim as a prophet. So do Jews and Christians, who know him as Abraham. Ibrahim lived over 2,000 years before the birth of Jesus.

Ibrahim about to sacrifice his son

Yasmin's Story

I am a Muslim. I remember how my father whispered the words of the *Adhan*, our daily prayer, to my new baby brother. During our Id-ul-Adha festival, or "Feast of Sacrifice," we remember Ibrahim. Because of his story, Muslim boys are circumcised. Our prophet Ibrahim is known to Jews and Christians as Abraham.

Muslim Birth Customs

Muslim babies are named when they are seven days old, at a ceremony called *Aqiqah*. The name is often one of Allah's 99 names with "Abd" added. Abdullah means "servant of God." The baby's head is shaved and in many ceremonies baby boys are circumcised, that is, the foreskin of the penis is cut away.

The Aqiqah ceremony.

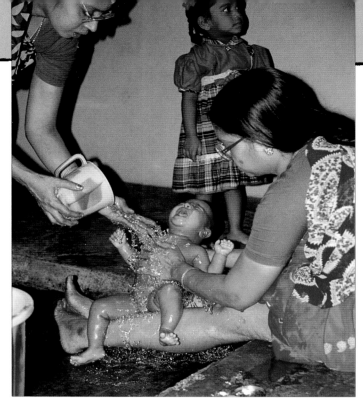

In preparation for the fourth *samsara*, the baby is washed. Then the Hindu symbol, *Aum*, is written on the baby's tongue with a golden pen dipped in honey.

Buddhist Birth Customs

When a baby is born to a Buddhist family in Thailand, the umbilical cord is placed in a clay pot and buried beneath a tree. Special objects are placed in the baby's cradle: books and tools for a boy, or needles and threads for a girl. After a month the baby's hair is cut. Sacred threads are tied around the wrists. Buddhist monks may be asked to give the child its name.

Hindu Birth Customs

The fourth Hindu ritual, or *samsara*, takes place at birth. (The first three take place before birth.) The newborn baby is washed and the sacred symbol, *Aum*, is traced on the tongue. The baby is named 12 days later. First a horoscope (a forecast for the future) is worked out. A boy may be called Vjaya, meaning "Victory." A girl may be called Kumari, which means "Princess."

Jewish Birth Customs

Jewish baby boys are circumcised at eight days of age. The ceremony is called *Brit Milah* or "Ceremony of Cutting." It symbolizes Abraham's covenant with God. The mother is not present. The baby is held by a male relative called a *sandek*. Then the baby is given a taste of sweet wine and there is a celebratory meal.

A Brit Milah ceremony.

The Hindu sacred symbol, *Aum*, means everything that ever was, is now, and will be. Hindus repeat it to themselves as they pray.

Ceremonies

Your first name—called by Christians your "Christian" name—is your identity. Roman Catholic parents may name a baby after a relative and after a saint (a holy person), so the baby has two or more "first" names. Many names have a special meaning.

Chinese children are finally named at age seven.

Chinese Full Month Feast

Each culture has a naming day ceremony. In China babies are not given any name until they are a month old. Even then it is just a nickname, so that bad spirits will not be jealous. A real name is not given until the child is seven years old. At the Full Month naming ceremony guests are offered lucky red eggs. They give the baby new clothing. Long ago a "hundred families coat" was a popular gift, made from scraps of cloth from family and friends.

The 12 animal signs in the Chinese horoscope are: Snake, Horse, Ram, Monkey, Rooster, Dog, Pig, Rat, Ox, Tiger, Rabbit, and Dragon.

Chinese Birth Years

Chinese babies have their horoscope read at birth. The year of birth is associated with a particular animal sign. A 12-year cycle is repeated. Each animal has its own character. 1999 was the Year of the Rabbit. The rabbit's characteristics are calmness, imagination, and generosity. 2000 was the Year of the Dragon. The dragon is strong and full of energy.

Christian Baptism

Most Christian babies are named at a ceremony called a Christening. This service welcomes the baby into the Church and happens around the font. Holy water may be used to mark the sign of the cross on the baby's forehead. Parents and godparents promise to teach the child about Christianity. They light candles to symbolize how God brought light to the world.

At baptism, Roman Catholic babies are given their names. The first name is often a saint's name.

African Naming Days

Various naming customs take place all over Africa. In North and West Africa many people follow Muslim naming traditions. The Yoruba people of Nigeria name their babies eight days after birth. In Ghana, names are given according to the day of the week the baby is born. So a boy or girl born on Wednesday will be named Ekua, the Ghanaian word for "Wednesday"; if they are born on Friday the name will be Kofi.

This mother and her little boy live in Nigeria, West Africa. Many Nigerians follow Muslim naming traditions.

African Names

Names given by Ndebele parents in South Africa have special meanings. A popular name is Thandi, which means "Hope" in the Ndebele language. In Cameroon, young Dowayo boys receive a new name after circumcision. A name gives a person an identity. African slaves were not allowed to use their names, because they were treated as property, not people with their own identities.

Kayapo People

In the Amazon rainforest in South America, Kayapo boys have a naming ceremony that lasts weeks. They are given the names of their ancestors. The boys wear jewelry and elaborate headdresses. Their bodies are covered with bright parrot feathers and their faces with crushed eggshells.

Making Trouble Dolls

In Guatemala in Central America, children make trouble dolls. They tell their worries to the dolls and put them under their pillows. The children believe that while they sleep, the dolls carry away their troubles.

1. Use paints to draw a face, hair and feet on each wooden clothes peg.
2. Ask an adult to cut a notch in each side of the clothes pegs then glue popsicle-stick halves into the notches to make the dolls' arms.
3. Wind yarn around the pegs. Wind some more across the arms to make the dolls' woollen capes.

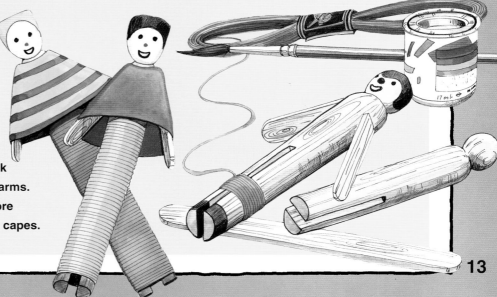

Growing Up

Birthdays are turning points in our lives. In most of the Western world, when young people reach their 18th birthday they know they are officially adults, because the law says so. They can vote and can decide to get married. In many societies, coming-of-age rituals take place.

Birthday Parties

Every birthday is special. Before a birthday party, invitations are written and decorations are hung. At a party there are games to play and treats to eat. All the cake's candles must be blown out, while guests sing *Happy Birthday*. Best of all, there are presents and cards. French and Greek children also celebrate their name days, by giving sweet cakes to their friends.

Balloons make a birthday party go with a bang!

Lionel's Story

I look forward to being 13. It is a special birthday for all Jewish boys. I will have my Bar Mitzvah in the synagogue. This is the "growing-up" ceremony for Jewish boys. My sister, who is almost 12, will have her growing-up ceremony this year. It is called Bat Mitzvah. It means "daughter of the commandment." Not all Jewish girls have a Bat Mitzvah.

Bar Mitzvah

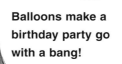

Bar Mitzvah, the coming-of-age ceremony for Jewish boys, is held in synagogue on the first Sabbath after his 13th birthday. This follows two years of religious teaching. During the ceremony the boy reads from the Jewish holy scroll, the *Torah*. He accepts a prayer shawl, or *tallit*, made of silk or wool, and a prayer book, or *siddur*. He thanks the grown-ups and receives presents at the party that follows.

Reading from the Torah at my bar mitzvah.

Confirmation

Roman Catholic children are welcomed into the Church when they are seven or eight and have their First Communion. Girls dress up in white and boys wear formal suits. Then they attend classes to learn more about Christianity. Confirmation happens on a Sunday when the children are 13 to 15 years old. Afterward they can take holy communion. They receive a wafer of bread and sometimes a sip of wine. With them, believers "receive" the body and blood of Jesus.

Someone who has been confirmed can take holy communion. The priest or minister gives the believer a wafer of bread. Then the believer takes a sip of wine from a communal, or shared, silver goblet.

This Hindu boy wears a beautiful garland of orange flowers for his Sacred Thread Ceremony.

The Last Supper

The ceremony of holy communion is also known as the eucharist or mass. It is linked with Easter. It recalls Jesus' last supper with his disciples, or followers, during the Jewish festival of Passover. When he sat down to the meal, Jesus knew that he would soon die. During this "Last Supper" they shared unleavened bread (bread made without yeast) and wine. Jesus asked his disciples to drink the wine and eat the bread in remembrance of him.

Hindu Sacred Thread

The tenth *samsara* for most Hindu boys is called the *Upanayana*, or "Sacred Thread Ceremony." A thread with three or five strands is hung over the shoulder of each boy. The strands symbolize the debts the boys owe to God and to their elders. The strands are tied together with a *brahma granthi* or spiritual knot. The boys each receive a student stick, to show they are ready to learn about Hinduism. Afterward they have ritual baths, to mark a new beginning.

Dressing Up

Young people look forward to the time when they are accepted as grown-ups. An initiation can be a special ritual or a simple ceremony. To mark the occasion, young people often wear a special costume.

Baisakhi (April)

Sikh children the age of 14 are initiated into the *khalsa* (Sikh community) during the festival of Baisakhi. Each must have the five Ks, which are symbols of their faith. The five Ks are *kesh* (uncut hair), *kangha* (a comb), *kirpan* (a dagger), *kacchera* (shorts), and *kara* (a bracelet). The children drink a sweet drink called *amrit* and share a sweet food. To show that all Sikhs are part of the same community, boys are given the surname Singh, meaning "Lion"; girls take the surname Kaur, meaning "Princess."

This girl wears her best *kimono* for Shichi-go-san and visits the Meiji Jingu Shrine, in Tokyo.

Wrapping a Sikh Turban

The Sikh custom of *kesh* means that Sikhs are not permitted to cut their hair. Girls braid their hair or wear a scarf called a *chunni*. Boys learn how to tie a *turban*, which is a long length of cloth.

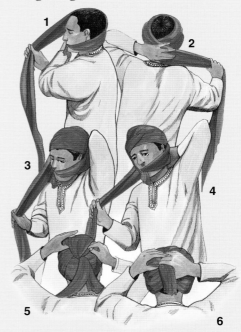

1. The hair is secured with the *kanga*, or comb. One end of the cloth is gripped in the teeth.
2, 3, 4. The rest of the cloth is wound around the head and pulled to tighten it.
5. The end of the cloth is tucked into the top.
6. Finally, the end being held by the teeth is tucked in.

Shichi-go-san (November 15)

On November 15 some Japanese families celebrate Shichi-go-san, which means "seven-five-three." This is a special day for girls aged 7, boys aged 5, and all 3-year-olds. Children dress up in their best clothes and visit the Shinto shrine with their parents. At the shrine, they say prayers for their good health. The Shinto priest blesses the children and gives them a sweetmeat that symbolizes health and a long life.

Growing up in Africa

Many African peoples hold initiation ceremonies for youths. Most are circumcision rituals. In North Cameroon, young men of the Dowayo people dress up in animal skins and are sent away from their community for some weeks before the ceremony. Afterward they wear traditional wickerwork cones that cover their bodies. They are said to be reborn and are given new names. Boys in Papua New Guinea take part in a similar ceremony.

In Papua New Guinea, southeast Asia, children wear face and hair paint and beaded clothes for special ceremonies.

Buddhist Monks

Young Thai boys spend a few months living as Buddhist monks to learn about their religion. Beforehand, a boy's head is shaved and he is dressed in white. Then dancers lead the boy to the monastery. There he makes vows, or promises, to lead a simple life. He changes into the colored robes of a novice, or learner, monk and gives flowers or gifts to the other monks.

First Day at School

The first day at a new school is both exciting and strange. It may involve wearing a new school uniform or being given a new backpack or a computer. In St. Petersburg, Russia, new pupils at the school of ballet arrive bearing huge bunches of flowers for their teachers. In Germany, parents give children starting school a big paper cone filled with candies and cookies.

Novice Buddhist monks have their heads shaved and wear yellow, orange, or red robes. At the monastery, the novices help the monks with daily tasks.

These children in England are dressed in uniforms to start their new school.

17

Wedding Celebrations

Weddings celebrate love and commitment. Couples exchange promises or vows at their wedding. A long time ago, royal Aztec couples made their vows by sharing a cup of chocolate. At a Japanese wedding, Shinto followers tell of a god and goddess who came down from heaven to be husband and wife.

Rama and Sita

Prince Rama was a reincarnation, or rebirth, of the god Vishnu. Rama and his wife Sita were sent to live alone for 14 years. Sita was captured by a ten-headed demon, Ravana. The monkey god, Hanuman, helped Rama to free Sita. Sita was unfairly accused of betraying Rama and was sent away. Then she gave birth to Rama's twin sons. At last Rama and Sita were reunited.

Gita's Story

My sister is getting married. My parents arranged the marriage with the groom's parents. Now everyone is very busy with the preparations. The ceremony will take place in our temple. All this excitement has made me think about the Indian love story of Rama and Sita. We usually tell this story during our Divali celebrations.

A Hindu Wedding

A Hindu bride decorates her hands and feet with *henna*. She puts on a red and gold wedding *sari* and gold jewelry. A grain of rice is placed on a holy mark on her forehead. The ceremony is under a *mandap*, or canopy, before a sacred flame. The couple, joined by a white cord, take seven steps around the flame. Prayers are said and the couple give each other garlands.

An Outdoor Wedding

In sunny places couples may decide to hold their wedding outdoors. Some couples marry on a tropical island. In Australia, weddings often take place in the garden. A Christian or Jewish outdoor wedding can still be a traditional white wedding, but sometimes the couple wear more casual clothes instead.

A guard of honor for a soldier groom and his bride.

The Jewish bride and groom stand under the flower-decorated *chuppah*, or canopy, in the synagogue.

Dowries

A dowry, or "bride-price," is traditionally brought by a bride to her husband. Today, this usually means that the bride's parents pay for the wedding, as happens in India and much of the West. Muslim grooms give dowries called *nikah* to their future bride's family. In Papua New Guinea, dowries are given to help keep the peace between different communities. Once, whole pigs and shells were given. Today, it might be strips of cooked pork, or pots and pans.

At many Hindu, Sikh, and Muslim weddings, the bride and groom wear garlands and colorful clothes like these.

A Jewish Wedding

Jewish marriages were once arranged by a matchmaker, or *shadkan*. The bride wears white and the ceremony usually takes place on a Sunday in the synagogue. The couple sip wine as the rabbi blesses them. The groom places a gold ring on his bride's finger. Seven more blessings are given. Then the bridegroom breaks a glass under his foot to symbolize the sad side of life.

19

Dressing Up

Wedding celebrations bring the fun of dressing up in special clothes. At traditional Christian or Jewish weddings, girls who are friends or relations of the couple dress up as bridesmaids. Boys dress up as page-boys. The bride often wears white. Eastern brides wear more colorful clothes.

Christian Wedding

A traditional Christian wedding is announced in church three times before the wedding day. The ceremony takes place in the church, usually on a Saturday. The couple makes their vows in front of the priest and usually exchange rings. The bride often wears a white dress and veil, and carries a bouquet. Sometimes the couple signs a register before leaving the church. Outside, the guests shower the couple with confetti. After the wedding meal and party, the couple goes away together on honeymoon.

Muslim Wedding

Before a Muslim wedding, gifts of jewelry and fabrics are exchanged. A simple ceremony can happen in the mosque or in the home. The bride wears trousers and a tunic, called her *shalwar* and *khameez*. She agrees three times to the marriage, then the groom signs a marriage contract. The bride's family provides a wedding feast.

Rings on their Fingers

An engagement ring symbolizes a promise to marry. The bride and groom exchange rings when they marry, to symbolize faithfulness and eternity.

Greek Orthodox Wedding

During a Greek Orthodox wedding ceremony in church, the bride and groom wear crowns joined by red ribbons. The wedding feast afterward is a lively affair with lots of music and dancing. The newly-weds dance together joined by a white scarf. At the end, guests pin money to the couple's clothes to give them a start as they begin their new life together.

Zulu Beads

Zulu girls send "love letters" made of colored beads to boys they like. White beads stand for purity and truth. Red ones mean love. Yellow stands for a home, while green means married happiness. Blue is for faithfulness. Tassels of these beads are hung from a length of white beads to form individual "love letters."

This Japanese couple pose for a wedding photo with their families near the entrance to the shrine.

Special Foods

After the wedding ceremony comes the wedding feast. This may be called a reception or a banquet—whatever the name, the meaning is the same. It is a happy occasion when families and friends sit down and share food.

In Burma, a Buddhist bride and bridegroom share food from the same silver bowl during their wedding ceremony. This is to show that now they share everything.

At the center of a Western wedding feast is the cake. At some weddings, people eat pink-, white-, or silver-colored sugared almonds as a symbol of a sweet life.

A Sikh wedding couple visit first the bride's and then the groom's home to receive symbolic sweetmeats.

Traditional beaded clothing shows whether a Ndebele woman is married or single.

African Customs

A Ndebele bride wears a sheepskin cape (a *linaga*) decorated with white beads, a *jocolo* apron, and two long strips covered with white beads (a *nyoga*). She carries a wedding stick, a fertility doll, a gourd, and small baskets. During the ceremony she remains beneath a blanket. A married woman wears a different apron, called a *mapoto*. A Masai woman who is married wears lots of head and neck ornaments.

Special Days

Every country has its own national day to celebrate its achievements. Some hold independence day celebrations to remember when they first stood alone as a nation. These days are often national holidays, too.

Chinese Kite Festival

The Chinese have flown kites for over 3,000 years. Chinese paper kites are now made in the shape of fish, birds, and insects. The ninth day of the ninth month is the "Climbing the Heights" kite festival. It is named after a man who climbed high to escape disaster.

Hideo's Story

Every year in Japan there is a kite festival on Boys' Day, which we call Kodomono-hi. I love to watch the kites flying above the rooftops and to see the grown-ups playing tricks on each other and trying to bring down other kites! We fly big, carp-shaped kites. A carp is a type of fish that struggles upstream. This symbolizes the difficult journey through life.

Kodomono-hi

On May 5 Japanese boys enjoy Kodomono-hi, when carp kites are flown. The boys display warrior dolls called *samurai* that symbolize strength. The boys bathe in iris leaves and wear traditional costumes called *hakama*. Special rice cakes are eaten.

Hina Matsuri (March 3)

Every Japanese girl has a set of dolls that she gives to her husband when she marries. On March 3, girls dress up in a traditional *kimono* to look like their dolls. This is Hina Matsuri, or "Girls' Day." During a special ceremony at the Shinto shrine all bad luck is passed onto other dolls. These are carried to the sea in small wooden boats. People follow the procession, chanting prayers. Each boat is piled high with dolls and the flotilla is sent out to sea. Tasty treats such as pink rice cakes are eaten.

Hina **means "small doll" in Japanese. Girls display their dolls on stands draped with red cloth.**

On April 1, French children have fun trying secretly to pin paper fish onto their friends' backs.

April Fools' Day

April 1 is April Fools' day, a day when people play tricks. A television station once fooled people with a report on the Italian "spaghetti harvest." Of course, spaghetti is made from wheat and does not grow on trees, but some people believed the story! In France the day is known as Poisson d'avril, or "April fish." People make paper fish and try to pin them on their friends' backs—without getting noticed!

American Thanksgiving (November)

On the fourth Thursday in November, Americans sit down to their Thanksgiving feast of roast turkey and pumpkin pie. They give thanks for the harvest gathered by the Pilgrims who settled in America in 1621. The Pilgrims sat down together with local Native Americans for the first Thanksgiving meal. The Native Americans had shown the first settlers how to catch wild turkeys and how to grow sweetcorn, sweet potatoes, pumpkins, and cranberries.

People say *Grace* to thank God for their Thanksgiving meal.

Giving Presents

Everyone likes to receive cards and gifts on their birthday. But there are other special days when we can show how much we appreciate someone we love by giving them a card and a gift. This might be a relative, such as a mother or brother, or even a boyfriend or girlfriend. Some of these days have their origins in the distant past.

Mothers' Day

English Christians used to visit their "mother" church once a year on the fourth Sunday in Lent. This day was called Mothering Sunday. Now on this day, children give their mothers cards and flowers to thank them for all their love and care. In France, children honor their mothers at the Fête des Mères (Festival of Mothers), on the last Sunday in May.

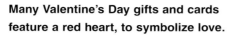

Many Valentine's Day gifts and cards feature a red heart, to symbolize love.

St. Valentine's Day (February 14)

On St. Valentine's Day, young men and women exchange love tokens. This custom has nothing to do with the Christian holy man, St. Valentine, although it happens on his feast day. It may be held in February because the Roman goddess Februa looked after marriage. Or it may simply be because February means spring is near. Long ago people gave love tokens, such as gloves and spoons. Nowadays people have fun by sending cards—signed or unsigned—to those they love.

People often give presents of jewelry, money, books, pens, or CDs for birthdays, Valentine's Day, and other special celebrations.

Raksha Bandhan (August)

Every August, Indian brothers and sisters show that they love each other during Raksha Bandhan, which means "bond of protection." The festival remembers the lucky bracelet that the god Indra's wife gave him to protect him in battle. In Hindu homes a ceremony called *puja* is performed on the morning of Raksha Bandhan. The sister makes a mark on her brother's forehead, then ties a bracelet, called a *rakhi*, to his wrist. He gives her a small gift, too, and they share some sweets.

The sister ties the *rakhi* around her brother's wrist. He then promises to protect her.

Making the Tilak Mark

Before tying the *rakhi* to her brother's wrist, a sister blesses her brother and makes a holy mark, or *tilak*, on his forehead. This is made with a red paste. Then she places a grain of rice on top of the *tilak*. This mark symbolizes success.

Make a Rakhi Bracelet

Rakhi bracelets are usually made from silk or cotton, but you can make your own *rakhi* from paper.
1. Decorate a wide strip of paper with red or gold shapes.
2. Braid together lengths of red and gold thread.
3. Attach the braided threads to holes in the ends of the paper strips.
4. Tie your *rakhi* around your wrist.

25

Lights and Fires

Leaping bonfires, fizzing fireworks, glowing lanterns, and flickering candles are at the center of the fun on many special days. The Chinese have used fireworks to frighten off demons for thousands of years. Flames are symbols of cleansing and rebirth. Fires and lanterns often represent the Sun and Moon, and many special days began as ancient acts of worship of a Sun god or a Moon goddess.

Fiesta week in Valencia is a colorful affair.

Halloween (October 31)

Halloween began as Samhain, the Celtic New Year. On this night, bonfires were lit to scare away ghosts and witches. Now, on November 1, Christians remember the dead. This is All Saints' Day, or All Hallows. Hallows means "holy." Halloween, the evening before All Hallows, is a time of fun. Children dress up as ghosts and vampires and play "trick or treat." Spooky, hollowed-out pumpkins called jack-o'-lanterns are lit up inside with candles.

Las Fallas (March 13–19)

In Spanish-speaking countries a *fiesta* is a Saint's Day. In Valencia, Spain, the *fiesta* week Las Fallas honors St. Joseph, whose feast day is March 19. There are fireworks and parades. Giant papier-mâché effigies (models of people) called *ninots* are stuffed with fireworks and burned.

A flickering candle inside a jack-o'-lantern is believed to keep away bad spirits.

These pumpkins have been made to look like witches.

Hola Mohalla (March)

Sikhs celebrate Hola Mohalla at the same time as Hindus celebrate Holi, to mark the arrival of spring. People squirt each other with colored water called *gulal*. The first Hola Mohalla was at Anandpur, when the tenth *guru* staged pretend battles to show off the skills of his soldiers. Today there is a fair at Anandpur for Hola Mohalla, where Sikhs light fires and show off their sporting prowess. On the last day Sikhs attend their place of worship, the *gurdwara*. Afterward they share holy food called *karah parshad*.

Sikhs light a huge bonfire for Hola Mohalla.

Holi festival (March)

Holi is a two-day festival in north India that celebrates the coming of spring. It is named after the demon, Holika. She tried to burn Prahlad, a follower of Vishnu, but she was burned instead. On the first day of Holi everyone has fun squirting colored water or sprinkling colored powders. Bonfires are lit on the second day to get rid of bad spirits. Then there is a feast.

Hindus spray each other with colored water for their springtime festival, Holi.

Children wear animal masks for Trung Thu.

Trung Thu (Autumn)

The Vietnamese Moon festival takes place on the 15th day of the eighth lunar month, to honor the Moon. Children wear masks and carry lanterns in a nighttime parade. Candles flicker inside the star-shaped lanterns, beneath the full Moon.

Boat races and picnics

Some special days involve energetic activities such as boat races, parades, and dancing. Some, like the Chinese Dragon Boat festival, have their origins in ancient stories. Others, such as London's Notting Hill Carnival, have developed more recently, from a mix of different cultures. All these special days have one thing in common—it is great fun to celebrate in the fresh air.

At Duan Yang, red, blue, and gold boats, each with a dragon's head on the prow, race to the beat of drums. In the evening there is a lantern-lit flotilla.

Duan Yang (June)

This is the Chinese Dragon Boat Festival. It celebrates the story of Qu Yuan, a kindly Chinese poet who lived 2,500 years ago. He wanted to help the poor. When he failed, he drowned himself. People tried to save him with their dragon boats, but were too late. They threw rice dumplings into the water to keep dragons and demons from his body. Rice dumplings are eaten during Duan Yang and dragon boats are raced.

May Day (May 1)

The Celts celebrated Beltane in May to mark the return of the Sun and the beginning of summer. They lit bonfires and decorated trees. The Romans had a similar celebration to worship Flora, the goddess of flowers, when they decorated trees with flowers. In medieval times May Day traditions such as dancing around the maypole and riding a hobby-horse began. In France on May Day, people give one another a bouquet of lily-of-the-valley.

The maypole's ribbons wind around the pole as the young people dance.

Cherry Blossom Viewing (April)

In the first week of April, cherry trees bloom all over Japan. Each region begins their Flower Viewing Festival when the blossoms open. The blossom is a symbol of hope and pride. Some of the loveliest cherry blossoms can be seen at Shinto shrines or on holy mountains. Families have fun in their local parks. They have picnics and drink rice wine.

Breton ladies traditionally wore tall hats made from beautiful lace.

Families take a picnic to the park to enjoy the cherry blossoms.

Pont l'Abbe Hat Festival (June)

Ladies in Brittany, France, used to wear tall lace hats. In June 1993 the last festival of Breton hats took place at Pont l'Abbe. Elderly ladies, called *bigoudenes*, wore their hats. The tradition ended because no young women are willing to carry it on. The hats used to be worn at the Pardon, a festival when everyone walked in procession to church to pray for forgiveness.

Notting Hill Carnival

For a weekend every August, the streets of Notting Hill, London, resound to the beat of *calypso* music. This carnival was begun by settlers from Trinidad in 1966 and resembles the Caribbean Mardi Gras carnivals. It is a street party and a happy social event for all. Fantastic costumes and floats move in procession through the streets. Dancers move to the rhythms of steel pans. Children join in too, dressed in elaborate carnival costumes.

At the Notting Hill Carnival, people wear colorful clothes and make lots of noise!

Ceremonies

Historic events are passed on to the next generation through the rituals performed for celebrations. Children can learn about the past from their parents and grandparents. Many festivals have ancient origins. The opening ceremony for the Olympic Games has its origins in the distant past of Ancient Greece. The Italian festival called Palio began in medieval times.

American Independence Day (July 4)

After many years of argument and conflict between the colonists and their British rulers, the Americans started to rebel. On July 4, 1776, the colonists issued the *Declaration of Independence*, which started a seven-year war that did lead to them breaking free from Britain. July 4 is now a United States' national holiday. There are parades, pageants, firework displays, and, of course, picnics and parties.

Children in the United States display their national flag on Independence Day.

The Olympic Games

The first Olympics took place over 2,500 years ago in Greece to honor the god Zeus. Now, every four years there is an international celebration of sport called the Olympic Games. A different city hosts the event each time. Sydney in Australia hosted the games in 2000. At the grand opening ceremony, athletes carry their national flags in a spectacular parade.

An everlasting flame is carried all the way from Greece to light the Olympic torch at the start of the Games.

The Palio (July/August)

Crowds of spectators attend the Palio twice each year. This bareback horse race around the Piazza del Campo in Siena, Italy, dates back over 600 years. Entrants come from the different *contradas* (districts) of Siena. Ten riders compete, often wearing medieval costumes. The prize is the *pallium*, a banner of the Virgin Mary.

The German Oktoberfest recalls the engagement of a Bavarian prince in 1810.

Competitors in the Siena Palio wear colorful costumes and riding hats.

National Days

Many countries celebrate a national day, when the nation's flag is flown and people wear traditional costume. For some, this is an independence day, a celebration of self-rule. The Inuit held their first Independence Day on April 1, 1999. Other festivals, such as the German Oktoberfest held each October, recall a special event.

Norwegian traditional dress

Norwegian National Day (May 17)

Norway's National Day is children's day. At schools, the Norway flag is hoisted at 8 a.m., and from 9 a.m. children, teachers, and parents meet wearing traditional dress or best clothes. Bands march and play the national anthem, and children, carrying small flags, march in procession behind the bands. This is called *Barnetoget*. Back at school there are speeches, songs, and games. Families go home for lunch or eat out. The children eat ice cream and sweets and drink lemonade. Some towns have another parade in the afternoon—the *Folketoget*—in which people march behind the banners of organizations. The partying goes on well into the night.

Memorial Days

On memorial days we celebrate but we also take time to contemplate. We remember those who gave their lives for our country. There are solemn parades at war memorials, such as the Tomb of the Unknown Soldier beneath the Arc de Triomphe in Paris.

Veteran's Day

The First World War ended in 1918 at the 11th hour on the 11th day of the 11th month. This day, once called Armistice Day, is now observed each year as Veteran's Day in the United States and as Remembrance Day in Canada. In Britain, Remembrance Day is held on the Sunday closest to November 11. There are services at war memorials. Armed forces march past and wreaths are laid to honor soldiers that died in the war.

Bernadette's Story

The First and Second World Wars (in 1914–18 and 1939–45) were major events in history. I have learned all about them in my history lessons. We visited the graves of soldiers who fought in the wars and died in France. Each year, a Remembrance Day ceremony is held in Paris at the Arc de Triomphe.

Poppies for Remembrance

Many people wear red poppies on Remembrance Day. That is because those flowers sprang up among the makeshift graves where soldiers were buried during the First World War.

The graves were among the muddy trenches in the fields of northern France and Belgium. Soldiers of many different nationalities died there.

Each year a Remembrance Day ceremony is held at the Arc de Triomphe, in Paris.

Wesak or Vesakha (May/June)

On the full Moon of Wesak, Buddhists pay respect to their founder, Buddha. Buddha was a man called Siddhartha Gautama. It was on the full Moon of Wesak that he finally understood life's meaning. Buddhists call this "enlightenment." Wesak is a happy day of prayer, when people remember Buddha's birth, enlightenment, and death. They send each other greeting cards and decorate homes and temples with lanterns.

People light candles for Wesak.

These Buddhists light candles to celebrate Wesak and remember Buddha.

These Jewish children are wearing fancy dress as part of the celebrations for Purim.

Yom Ha-Shoah (January 29)

Yom Ha-Shoah is a remembrance day in Israel. It is a quiet day of contemplation. The evening before, all public entertainment stops as a mark of respect. On this day Jews remember the Holocaust (or *Shoah*) that happened during the Second World War. *Shoah* means "burnt sacrifice." About six million Jews were killed in gas chambers by the Nazis because of their faith.

Purim (March)

Purim is a one-day Jewish memorial festival. On this day, Jews go to synagogue to hear the story of a plot to kill the Jews in Persia (Iran). Children dress up and whenever they hear the villain's name, Haman, they hiss and boo loudly. Haman wanted to kill all Jews after a Jew called Mordecai refused to bow to him. But the Jewish queen Esther saved her people from Haman.

33

Parades

On memorial days we think about people and events that have made the world a better place to live in. We remember special people and celebrate their achievements.

Bastille Day (July 14)

During the French Revolution (1789–99) people fought for their freedom. In Paris, the Bastille prison stood for all that poor people hated. On July 14, 1789, a mob of hungry, angry Parisians broke in and freed the prisoners. Today in France, July 14 is a national holiday. The day itself is quiet, but on the evening before there are big celebrations. Every town and village celebrates with a parade and fireworks display.

These riders are carrying the United States flag, the Stars and Stripes on Memorial Day.

In 1789 French revolutionaries stormed the Bastille prison in Paris.

Memorial Day (May)

On the last Monday in May people in the United States hold processions and listen to speeches in memory of those in the armed forces who died for their country. It used to be called Decoration Day, because war graves were decorated with flowers and flags. The first ceremony, in 1868, was in memory of those who died in the Civil War (1861–1865).

New Zealand children wear their scouts uniform on Anzac Day. "Anzac" is from the first letters of Australian and New Zealand Army Corps.

Anzac Day (April 25)

Thousands of Australian and New Zealand soldiers died at Gallipoli, Turkey, in 1915. On Anzac Day people remember the dead. There are parades and children wear their grandparents' medals. Flags fly at half-mast. All is quiet as a bugler plays the *Last Post*.

St. Patrick's Day (March 17)

Patrick is Ireland's patron saint. He used the three-leaved shamrock plant to teach his followers about the Trinity—how God could be the Father, Son (Jesus), and Holy Spirit all at once. The Irish honor St. Patrick on March 17. They wear sprigs of shamrock.

Russians hold a big May Day parade in Red Square, Moscow.

Labor Day (early September)

In the United States and Canada, Labor Day is the first Monday in September. In many other parts of the world, May 1 is a holiday better known for workers' parades. This is because in 1890, May 1 was made International Workers' Day, or Labor Day. Many cities hold parades. In Russia and China, May Day celebrations usually involve large military parades through the capital cities, Moscow and Beijing.

Gandhi Jayanti (October 2)

Gandhi's lifelong wish for Indian independence came true on August 14, 1947. This is Indian Independence Day.

Mohandas Karamchand Gandhi (1869–1948) was a Hindu. He was shot by an assassin after a lifetime of peaceful resistance to British rule in India. Now Indians remember his birthday every year on October 2. Gandhi Jayanti is a national holiday.

In New York, where there is a large Irish community, people hold St. Patrick's Day parades.

Lights and Fires

Memorial celebrations can be joyous occasions. For Hindus, death is the beginning of a new life in another form. The Aztecs thought their dead came back as hummingbirds and butterflies. It is now traditional in Mexico to have fun on All Souls' Day, when the souls of the dead visit. Flowers are laid on the graves and flickering candles brighten these happy nighttime scenes.

Mexican Day of the Dead (November 1–2)

Mexicans enjoy All Souls' Day, or the Day of the Dead. They clean their family tombs, decorate them with flowers and candles, and spend the night there. Tables (*ofrendas*) are filled with offerings for the dead—perhaps their favorite foods or some belongings. During the day dancers wearing skull masks take part in *fiestas*.

In Mexico people make beautiful altars of offerings to the dead. These may be laden with flowers, candles, and food.

Making Sugar Skulls

These colorful, icing-sugar skulls will last for a long time.

On the Day of the Dead in Mexico, children enjoy special sweets, such as sugar skulls. You can make a delicious skull from fondant icing.

1. Add food coloring to some fondant icing.
2. With your fingers, mold the icing into a skull shape.
3. Make the features on the skull with a modeling tool.
4. Decorate your skull with edible cake decorations.

36

Guy Fawkes' Night (November 5)

On November 5, 1605, Guy Fawkes tried to blow up the British Parliament with gunpowder, but his plot failed. Ever since, British people have celebrated Guy Fawkes' Night, or Bonfire Night. Stuffed figures called *guys* are burned on big bonfires and there are firework displays.

On Bonfire Night, the skies of Britain are lit up with spectacular displays of fireworks.

The *kinara* holds seven candles that are black, green, and red. Each day during Kwanzaa another candle is lit.

Kwanzaa (December/January)

Kwanzaa is a week-long American celebration that includes many African cultural features. In rituals, poetry, singing, dancing, and feasting, black Americans remember their African ancestry. *Kwanzaa* means "first fruits" in Swahili, and the celebration began to mark a harvest festival of the first crops in Africa. Seven colored candles are lit, one each day starting on December 26, to symbolize the seven principles of Kwanzaa. The principles are based on Africans belonging to one family wherever in the world they live. In many families, parents and children exchange gifts, such as craftwork made in traditional African styles.

Each winter African Americans gather to celebrate Kwanzaa with candles, African music, and fruits.

Ceremonies

We owe our modern world to the efforts of our ancestors. The living show respect for their ancestors in ceremonies all over the world. Some ceremonies are ancient, religious rituals. Others are much more recent in origin.

Columbus Day (October 12)

Christopher Columbus reached the Caribbean in 1492. He claimed the land for Spain. Since 1792, the United States has celebrated Columbus Day every year on October 12, or the second Monday of the month. It is a public holiday. The first pledge of allegiance to the American flag was made on Columbus Day, 1892. In Colombia, South America, Colombians celebrate their Spanish ancestry on October 12, which they call *Dia de la Raza* (the Day of Race). Children perform plays about Columbus.

Each October, Colombians celebrate the Dia de la Raza. They remember the important influence of Spanish settlers on their culture and history.

Martin Luther King, Jr. Day (January)

Martin Luther King, Jr. was a black American clergyman. He spent his life campaigning peacefully for equal rights for black people. In 1964 he was awarded the Nobel Peace Prize, but he was shot in 1968. Now people in the United States celebrate Martin Luther King, Jr. Day on the third Monday in January, the Monday nearest his birthday. It is a national holiday.

School bands take part in the Martin Luther King, Jr. Day celebrations.

Passover (April)

Passover is a celebration that reminds Jews how their ancestors escaped from slavery in Egypt. Before Passover every Jewish home is spring-cleaned. The festival lasts eight days. On the first night is a special meal called *seder*. On the *seder* dish are symbolic Passover foods: an egg, parsley, horseradish, a roasted lamb bone, saltwater, and a sweet mixture called *charoset*. People also eat a flat bread called *matzoh* and everyone drinks wine.

Seder is the Passover meal.

Making Charoset

Charoset is a Passover treat that reminds Jews of the building mortar used by Jewish slaves in Ancient Egypt.

1. Peel, core and grate three apples.
2. Add half a cup of chopped walnuts, one tablespoon of chopped dates and raisins, and two tablespoons of apple juice.
3. Sprinkle on some ground cinnamon and mix everything together well.

Berlin Wall Party (November 9)

When the Second World War ended in 1945, Germany was split into two. Berlin was divided into East and West Germany. Families were separated and a wall was built. People who tried to cross the wall were shot. At last, in 1989, the Berlin Wall came down and Germany became one country again. In 1999, a decade later, a celebratory party was held at the Brandenburg Gate, which links the two halves of the city.

In 1989 Germans celebrated the fall of the Berlin Wall and the start of their one nation.

New Year

New Year celebrations are varied. Those who follow the Gregorian calendar celebrate on December 31, New Year's Eve. But Chinese New Year is a lunar calendar event, celebrated in late January or February. The Hindu New Year is in November, while Rastafarians celebrate New Year in September.

Janus

The month of January is named after the Roman god of new beginnings, Janus. Janus had two faces looking in opposite directions. His temple in Ancient Rome had two doors facing east and west. On the first day of *Januarius*, the 11th month of the Roman year, people made sacrifices to Janus. At New Year the door to the temple was opened, letting out the old year and the new year in.

The two faces of Janus outside the temple.

Grace's Story

I live in Memphis. I enjoy New Year because we have a family party with party poppers. I will make some New Year's Resolutions. I don't expect I will keep them all, but I will try very hard to stop arguing with my big brother. When I am older I will be allowed to stay awake until after midnight on New Year's Eve.

Times Square Party (December 31)

At the New Year's Eve party in Times Square, New York, neon lights flash and the smell of hot dogs fills the air. At midnight a huge shining ball of light is lowered from a flagpole on top of the Times Building. In 1999 a giant video screen showed the New York revellers other millennium parties around the world.

Millennium Party (December 31, 1999)

January 1, 2000, was a special day for Christians because the Gregorian calendar dates from the birth of Jesus over 2,000 years ago. Hindus, Muslims, and Jews all joined in the party, even though their religions have their own different calendars. For example, the Hindu year 2056 began on November 8, 1999. The Muslim calendar reached the year 1421 in the Gregorian year of 2000. And the Jewish calendar reached the year 5761 in 2000.

Fireworks exploded above Sydney, Australia, to mark the new millennium.

First footing is a Scottish New Year's Eve tradition.

Hogmanay

In Scotland, New Year's Eve is called Hogmanay. At midnight everyone sings *Auld Lang Syne*. Another Scottish custom at Hogmanay is called "first footing." On the last stroke of midnight a dark-haired man is invited in. He brings a lump of coal (so the house will be warm all year), bread (so there will always be food on the table), and a coin (so the family will not be poor).

New Year's Promises or Resolutions

At New Year people make promises to themselves. It is a time to make a new start. Here is Grace's list of resolutions. What would you put on your list?

1. I will stop quarreling and fighting with my brother.
2. I will make my bed and clean my bedroom every morning before school.
3. I will finish all my homework before I watch any television.
4. I will get out of bed right away when my alarm clock goes off.
5. I will not sneak treats from the kitchen when Mom and Dad aren't looking.

Parties

The Chinese New Year, Yuan Tan, is the first day of the first month of the lunar calendar. It is lavish and colorful. Chinese families spend a lot of time preparing for this celebration. This is also true in Vietnam, where the Tet Festival is the highlight of the year. The symbolism of colors, objects, and rituals is very important. Lucky citrus fruits are displayed. These ancient traditions are enjoyed by people of all ages.

Chinese New Year (January/February)

Chinese New Year celebrations last two weeks. First, the kitchen god is honored. Then the home is cleaned and people hang decorations. On New Year's Eve people light firecrackers. Everyone visits friends with gifts of food and drink. Children are given "lucky" money in red paper envelopes. Kumquats, oranges, and tangerines are displayed for good luck.

New Year celebration symbols and signs—a Chinese lantern, calendar, greetings card, and dragon puppet; a Jewish shofar; candles; wintertime decorations; colored paper streamers, chain, and hats; glitter; and a glass for champagne.

Lantern Festival (February/March)

The last day of the Chinese New Year is the Lantern Festival, Teng Chieh. This always happens on the first full Moon of the year. Homes and buildings are strung with glowing lanterns of all colors and shapes. The famous dragon and lion dancers weave their way through the crowded streets. The dragon is symbolic of long life and prosperity.

On the last day of Chinese New Year celebrations, dragon and lion dancers perform in the streets.

New Year's Eve (December 31)

Many families organize New Year's Eve parties for relatives and friends so they can celebrate New Year together. These parties go on past midnight. Guests play games and enjoy party foods and drinks. As the midnight-hour approaches, poppers, streamers, and horns are set off. On the stroke of midnight the noise is deafening as everyone cheers. Champagne corks pop. In Italy on this night it is traditional to throw old furniture and pots out of the window—if the streets are empty!

Tet Festival (February)

In Vietnam the New Year Tet Festival lasts seven days. Homes are decorated with a yellow blossom called *hoa mai*. A New Year's tree, or *cay neu*, stands outside to keep out bad spirits. It is bamboo decorated with red paper. Tangerine trees are displayed for good luck.

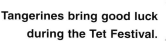

Tangerines bring good luck during the Tet Festival.

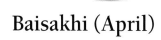

In 1999, Sikhs celebrated the 300th anniversary of the founding of the *khalsa*.

Baisakhi (April)

Sikhs in Punjab, north India, celebrate their new year, Baisakhi, in April. The Sikh flag is raised and there is feasting and dancing. At this time, Sikhs remember how Guru Gobind Singh (the tenth *guru*, or teacher) tested his followers. He asked who would die for their beliefs. Five men offered themselves. The *guru* gave them a sweet drink called *amrit*. This was how the Sikh brotherhood or *khalsa* was founded. Young men become full members of the khalsa at Baisakhi.

Ceremonies

New Year is celebrated in many different ways, and even at different times. But all New Years have something in common. They all symbolize a new beginning. New Year is the time to reflect on the year gone by. It is time to make changes.

Rosh Hoshanah (September)

Jewish New Year is called Rosh Hoshanah. It is a two-day holiday beginning on the first day of the Jewish month Tishri. Celebrations start at sunset, in the home. Two candles are lit. People drink wine and eat *challah* bread. They also eat pieces of apple dipped in honey, in the hope of a sweet new year. Jews believe that on this day Abraham prepared to sacrifice his son. New Year's Day is a quiet, serious occasion. The *shofar* (ram's horn) is blown in the synagogue. Jews think about the past year.

At Rosh Hoshanah, the rabbi blows the *shofar*, or ram's horn.

Tu b'Shevat (January/ February)

The 15th day of the month of Shevat is New Year's Day for trees in Israel. Tu b'Shevat marks the end of winter. Many children take part in tree-planting ceremonies. Trees symbolize new growth. Long ago, Jews used to plant a cedar tree when a baby boy was born, or a cypress for a baby girl. The trunks of these trees were used to make wedding tents when the babies became adults and got married.

In Israel, children plant trees for Tu b'Shevat. Trees are a gift to the people of the future because they take so many years to grow.

In Sikkim in India, Buddhist priests or *lamas* throw the world's troubles on to a bonfire.

Losar (January)

Tibet's Losar celebrations last three days. The first day is a family day. Then friends and relatives visit and exchange gifts. Tibetan homes are painted white outside and people wear new clothes. They decorate their family shrines with lucky charms such as ears of corn. People give offerings to Buddhist monks and perform special rituals to drive away evil spirits.

Setsubun (February)

The Japanese festival of Setsubun, or Bean Scattering, is held soon after the New Year, in February. This is a spring festival when evil spirits are driven out. On the family shrine stands a container holding beans. After dark, the eldest son of the family scatters the beans around the front door and in any dark corners. Over the doorway a small charm is hung to keep out bad spirits.

Songkran (April 12–14)

New Year in Thailand is called Songkran. There is a water festival with boat races and lots of splashing. A Songkran princess is appointed, who rides on a decorated wooden horse beneath a parasol. The festival ends with three drum beats and three rings of a bell.

Music is an important part of the joyful Thai New Year festival, Songkran.

The Bean Scattering ceremony takes place at household shrines and temples. Good luck for the new year is invited in. Beans symbolize good health and bring good luck.

Holy Days

A holy day is a religious festival. Sometimes a holy day celebrates a special event. The Jewish festival of Hannukah remembers when the Jews reclaimed their temple. Sometimes a holy day celebrates the life of someone special. Christians remember the birth of Jesus at Christmas. Today Christmas is a mixture of the traditions of many peoples in the northern part of the world. Each of them has their own midwinter celebration.

St. Nicholas

The story of Santa Claus began with St. Nicholas, or Sinter Klaus. He was a kind bishop who lived in Asia Minor in AD 300. Children came to believe that he would reward them if they were good. In Eastern Europe, on the eve of December 5, adults dress up as St. Nicholas and give treats to the children.

On December 6, Dutch people celebrate the festival of St. Nicholas, or Sinter Klaus. A grown-up dresses as a bishop and rides through the streets.

Sven's Story

I live in Sweden. Every year I look forward to Christmas, when Christians remember the birth of Jesus over 2,000 years ago. This is sometimes called the story of the Nativity. We decorate our homes with holly, ivy, and mistletoe. We light candles, send cards, and, best of all, exchange presents.

Christmas

The four weeks before Christmas are called Advent. At this time, Christians prepare to celebrate the birth of Jesus. Christmas Day is December 25 or, in Orthodox churches, January 6. For those who live in the southern hemisphere, it is a summer celebration.

On Christmas Eve, midnight masses are held in churches and cathedrals. On Christmas Day there is feasting and merrymaking. In some countries, December 26 is a celebration, the feast day of St. Stephen. This saint was the first Christian martyr, which means he died for his beliefs.

Fir trees are brought into homes and decorated. This tradition began in Germany about 1,000 years ago.

Singing Songs

Carols sung during Christmas are songs that tell the story of the birth of Jesus. They include *Silent Night*, *The First Nowell*, and *Away in a Manger*. Christmas carols are sung in churches. Groups of carol singers go out to entertain neighbors and friends. Traditionally this happens on Christmas Eve.

At some carol services, people hold candles to symbolize new life.

At a Christmas party, Father Christmas takes presents from his sack to give to the children.

Making Christmas Cards

Homemade Christmas cards are so much nicer than bought ones.

1. Take a piece of thin red paper 8 inches by 6 inches. Fold it in half and write your message inside.
2. Cut a tree shape from green paper.
3. Glue the tree on the front of the card.
4. Decorate the tree with stick-on stars.
5. Sprinkle the tree with glitter.

Giving Presents

Some children believe that Father Christmas, the English version of St. Nicholas, brings them gifts while they sleep on Christmas Eve. In Slovakia, children place a boot on the windowsill on the eve of December 5 in the belief that St. Nicholas will deliver them treats. These traditions remind Christians that baby Jesus received three gifts from the wise men.

Lights and Fires

Before there were electric lights or central heating, winters were dark and bitterly cold for people in the far north. They longed for spring and celebrated the return of the Sun after winter with bonfires and candle-light processions. Fire still features in religious winter festivals, symbolizing new beginnings. Christian Christmas, Jewish Hanukkah, and Hindu Divali are all festivals symbolized by lights.

We Hindus light oil lamps to invite the blessing of Lakshmi, our goddess of wealth.

Divali (October/November)

The Hindu festival of Divali is a celebration of good over evil and the start of the new year. The streets of India are alive with thousands of tiny lights, and Hindu homes everywhere sparkle in the glow of *diva* or electric fairy lights. Gifts and cards are exchanged. Special food is prepared and offered at the temple.

Divali guests are offered Indian sweetmeats, such as *barfi*, banana fudge, and *patashe*. Barfi, made from sugar, water, and milk powder, can be decorated with coconut, chopped nuts, or cherries.

For Divali, people draw patterns with colored rice at the front of their houses.

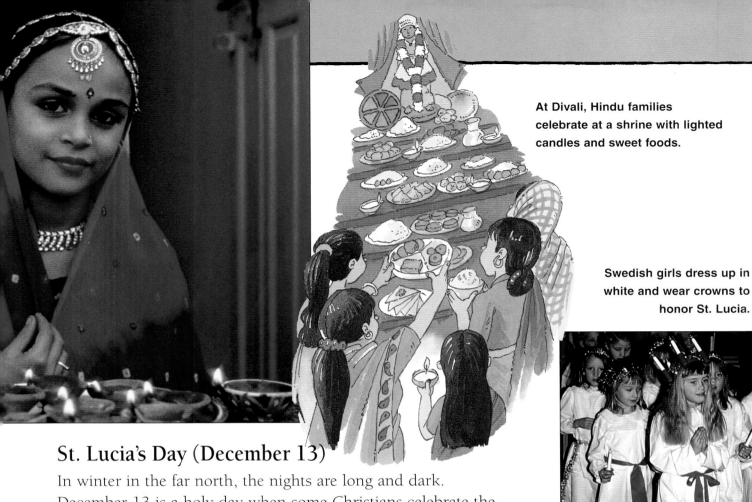

At Divali, Hindu families celebrate at a shrine with lighted candles and sweet foods.

Swedish girls dress up in white and wear crowns to honor St. Lucia.

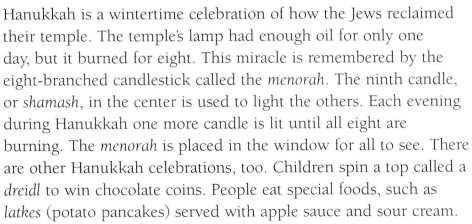

St. Lucia's Day (December 13)

In winter in the far north, the nights are long and dark. December 13 is a holy day when some Christians celebrate the feast day of St. Lucia, the patron saint of light. On this day, all over Sweden young girls wearing white dresses and evergreen crowns of candles lead processions in her honor. In Swedish homes, people eat special raisin-filled buns.

Hanukkah (December)

Hanukkah is a wintertime celebration of how the Jews reclaimed their temple. The temple's lamp had enough oil for only one day, but it burned for eight. This miracle is remembered by the eight-branched candlestick called the *menorah*. The ninth candle, or *shamash*, in the center is used to light the others. Each evening during Hanukkah one more candle is lit until all eight are burning. The *menorah* is placed in the window for all to see. There are other Hanukkah celebrations, too. Children spin a top called a *dreidl* to win chocolate coins. People eat special foods, such as *latkes* (potato pancakes) served with apple sauce and sour cream.

The *shamash*, or service candle, is used to light the other candles.

49

Parades and Races

Carnival is a time for extravagant costumes, musical parades, dancing, feasting, and fun. The Rio Carnival in Brazil, South America, is world famous and goes on for days. *Carnevale* means "farewell to meat." A long time ago carnival was an excuse for having some last fun before the Christian time of fast before Easter, called Lent. Buddhists also hold a holy day parade called Asalha Perahara. *Perahara* means "parade."

Early French settlers took Mardi Gras customs to the United States and the Caribbean.

Asalha Perahara (July/August)

Asalha Perahara is a Buddhist festival held in Kandy in Sri Lanka. On the night of the full Moon, there is a procession of over 100 elephants. One of the elephants carries the Buddha's tooth in a golden casket. There are dancers, acrobats, and jugglers, too.

Shrove Tuesday (February)

The last day before Christian Lent is Shrove Tuesday. "Shrove" is an old English word meaning "to be sorry." Christians go to church to say sorry for their sins in preparation for Lent. Many people make pancakes to use up their fatty foods (eggs and butter) before the fast. In France, Shrove Tuesday is called Mardi Gras, which is French for "fat Tuesday." In England, people hold pancake races in the streets, tossing the pancakes as they run.

This procession of amazing Mardi Gras floats took place in Nice, France.

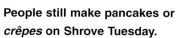

People still make pancakes or *crêpes* on Shrove Tuesday.

Dancers train all year for the Mardi Gras celebration. The preparations begin weeks in advance.

Each dancer has a costume made specially for the occasion and parades through the streets.

Some costumes are so elaborate that the dancer has to be carried through the streets on a float.

Mardi Gras (February)

Rio de Janeiro in Brazil has the biggest carnival of all. For five nights "schools" of costumed dancers parade through the streets. There is a competition to find the best dancers. Each country has its own carnival style. In New Orleans, in the United States, Mardi Gras lasts two weeks. People dress up as harlequins and jesters. In Trinidad, in the Caribbean, children wear amazing outfits and dance to the music of steel pans. The grown-ups hold a competition to elect a carnival king and queen.

Decorating costumes and floats can be expensive. But poor people can forget their troubles at carnival time.

Feasting and Fasting

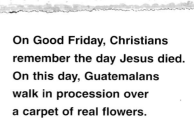

Days of fasting often come before days of feasting. This helps people to enjoy the feast more, and to think about what they are celebrating. Lent is when many Christians fast, before the happy time of Easter. Ramadan is the month of fasting for Muslims, before the festival of Id-ul-Fitr. Jews spend the day of Yom Kippur fasting, before the festival of Sukkot.

Holy Week in Guatemala (March/April)

After Lent comes the Christian Holy Week. Good Friday is the saddest day because that is when Jesus died. Hot cross buns symbolize his death on the cross. In Guatemala, Central America, Holy Week is called Semana Santa. On Good Friday, barefoot people dressed in purple carry a huge oak float, in silence, over a carpet of real flowers. On the float is a life-size figure of Jesus, in red, carrying a heavy wooden cross. People are sad as they think about Jesus' pain.

On Good Friday, Christians remember the day Jesus died. On this day, Guatemalans walk in procession over a carpet of real flowers.

Painted eggs and spring flowers are symbols of new life for Easter.

Easter Day (March/April)

Easter Day is always the Sunday nearest to the first full Moon after March 21. The date varies from year to year. It is named after Eostre, a pagan goddess of spring. Easter Day is a happy day, because Christians believe it is when Jesus rose from the dead. Church bells ring. Christians dress up in new clothes to attend flower-filled churches. The Easter story of Jesus coming alive again marks the beginning of Christianity. Children receive chocolate Easter eggs, because the egg is a symbol of new life.

Ramadan and Id-ul-Fitr

During the month of Ramadan Muslims remember how an angel first revealed the truths of the *Qur'an* to the Prophet Muhammad. People fast from just before dawn to just after dusk. When the new Moon rises, the *imam* (community leader) announces the fast is over. Then the three-day feast of Id-ul-Fitr begins. People share special foods, such as *samosas*, and they give each other cards and presents.

This horseback parade is part of the Muslim celebrations for Id-ul-Fitr.

Muslims celebrate the end of their Ramadan fast at Id-ul-Fitr.

Yom Kippur (September/October)

Ten days after Rosh Hoshanah is the quiet Jewish festival of Yom Kippur. Grown-ups do not eat or drink all day. The day is spent in synagogue asking forgiveness for the sins of the past year. The end of Yom Kippur is marked by the blowing of the *shofar*, a ram's horn.

In synagogue, the Jewish house of prayer, the shofar is blown at the end of the Yom Kippur service.

Following the Yom Kippur service in synagogue, people return home for an evening meal to end their fast.

53

Decorations

Harvest celebrations are mostly holy days. The time of harvest varies. In North America, harvest is in early fall. India's rice harvest is in January. All harvest festival decorations are symbols of thanks for Earth's products. People give thanks whether the harvest is a tropical crop, such as bananas, a temperate crop, such as apples, or even a harvest of fish from the sea.

In the Kiriwina Islands, in the Pacific Ocean, the chief crop is yams. These children are preparing to carry the yams to the harvest festival.

Harvest Festival

Harvest-time in Britain used to be much more special when most people lived in the countryside. Today most people live in towns and cities. But harvest thanksgiving services are still held in churches decorated with beautiful displays of fruits, vegetables, flowers, and loaves. Children bring foods that are given away after the service to the needy. In London, Pearly Kings and Queens dress up in clothes decorated with many buttons for a parade organized by local market traders.

Bread and ears of corn or wheat are often given pride of place at harvest festival celebrations. This is because the cereals are such important crops and because corn was a pagan symbol of fertility.

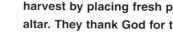

Christians in England celebrate the harvest by placing fresh produce on an altar. They thank God for their harvest.

Argungu (February/March)

Argungu, or the "Fishing Festival," has been celebrated in Nigeria, Africa, for over 400 years. It is held on the River Rima to mark the end of the fishing season. People wear clothes with fish patterns on them. There are sporting events. Of course, the most popular event is the fishing competition. Hundreds of men take part, using only a hollow gourd and two nets. The man who catches the largest fish receives a prize.

Jewish children decorate tents for Sukkot.

Sukkot (September/ October)

The Jewish fall-harvest festival is Sukkot. At this time of year, Jews remember how the Israelites wandered through the desert with Moses in search of the Promised Land. Children erect shelters or tents called *sukkot* in the garden. They decorate them with fruit and branches. Children also carry *lulav* (evergreen branches of palm or myrtle) as symbols of God's protection.

Shavuot (May/June)

Seven weeks after Passover, Jews celebrate their two-day spring-harvest festival, Shavuot. Shavuot reminds Jews of when Moses went up Mount Sinai and received the Ten Laws or Commandments from God. Long ago at Shavuot, people took the first crops of the harvest to the Temple in Jerusalem as an offering to God. Now synagogues are decorated with flowers and green branches. Children count off the days between Passover and Shavuot.

Everyone looks forward to Shavuot. In Israel, children sing and dance holding baskets of fruits and flowers.

Ceremonies

In pagan times people believed in Mother Earth and Father Sky. They gave thanks to Mother Earth at harvest-time. In Britain the corn dolly symbolized Mother Earth. In Peru a similar figure called Pirva was shaped from maize leaves. Hindus call Mother Earth Prithivi. The Ancient Greeks called her Gaia.

Dassehra honors the mother goddess, Durga.

Dassehra (September)

Dassehra is celebrated by Hindus in India at the end of the monsoon, the rainy season. Different forms of the goddess Durga are worshiped each night. Durga helped kill the demon king, Ravana. On the last day, a huge figure of the ten-headed Ravana, full of fireworks, is set on fire.

On the third day of Pongal, Hindus decorate their cattle.

Hindus make offerings of rice for Pongal.

Pongal (January)

Pongal is a Hindu festival held in India. On the first day, gifts of food, oil, or incense are carried to the temple. On the second day, gifts of sweets, fruits, and new rice are given. On the third and last day, cattle are honored and decorated with flowers. Cattle are sacred to Hindus. *Pongal*, a sweet made from rice, is eaten by everyone—including the cattle.

New Taste Festival (November 23)

Long ago in Japan, the new fall rice harvest could not be eaten until after a festival in honor of the rice spirit. There was dancing, singing, and waving of fans. Everyone enjoyed a great feast. Now that day is a national holiday and it takes place on November 23. The name has been changed to Labor Thanksgiving Day. At midnight the Japanese emperor offers the first fruits of fall at a special altar.

For the New Taste festival, people decorate shrines with fruits.

The Tree of Life

The Tree of Life features in the folk art of Mexico. There was a belief that the spirit of the trees could be captured by making use of bark and branches. Bark paper was made and turned into magic dolls. Harvest scenes were painted on bark paper. Today, colorful clay models of the Tree of Life are displayed. They often tell the story of Adam and Eve. These trees decorate churches in Mexico. A ceremony is held when a new tree of life is placed in a church.

The Tree of Life is always very intricate and brightly colored. This one shows Adam and Eve near the bottom, wearing fig leaves.

A Shared Calendar

The word calendar comes from the Greek *kalendae*, which means "to call" or "to proclaim." All calendars announce special dates. Religious calendars provide dates of holy days, but most people refer to the Gregorian calendar for ordinary daily events. So the Gregorian calendar is a shared calendar. But each country has its own unique culture and history, so certain dates are bound to be more special than others.

Celebrations of many religions such as Islam do not fall on set dates in the "everyday" calendar because they follow a lunar calendar.

All around the World

To prepare for religious celebrations, people refer to religious calendars. The Jewish calendar starts from the Creation. Dates are worked out from the movements of the Sun and the Moon. The Muslim calendar dates from AD 622. It is a lunar calendar.

Even if we measure time in different ways, we can still share our different celebrations. Modern life is now a colorful mixture of these shared differences.

January

1	New Year's Day (Gregorian calendar)
6	Epiphany (Christian)
6	Eastern Orthodox Christmas (Christian)
15	Seijin-no-hi/Adults' Day (Japan)
	Martin Luther King, Jr. Day (USA)
15–16	Pongal (Hindu)
25	Burns' Night (Scotland)
29	Yom Ha-Shoah (Israel)

January/February

Losar (Buddhist/Tibet)
Tu b'Shevat (Israel)
Yuan Tan/ Chinese New Year

February

2	Groundhog Day (USA)
3	Setsubun/Bean Scattering (Japan)
14	St. Valentine's Day
	MOVEABLE:
	Carnival (Christian)
	Shrove Tuesday/Mardi Gras (Christian)
	President's Day (USA)
	Tet Festival (Vietnam)

February/March

Argungu/Fishing Festival (Nigeria)
Teng Chieh/Chinese Lantern Festival

A tori gateway entrance to a Japanese shrine.

March

1	St. David's Day (Wales)
3	Hina Matsuri (Japan)
8	International Women's Day
13–19	Las Fallas (Valencia, Spain)
17	St. Patrick's Day (Ireland, USA)
19	St. Joseph's Day
	MOVEABLE:
	Hola Mohalla (Sikh)
	Holi (Hindu)
	Purim (Jewish)

March/April

Semana Santa (Christian/Guatemala)
Easter (Christian)
Mothering Sunday (UK)

April

1	April Fools' Day
1–8	Cherry Blossom Viewing (Japan)

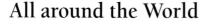

13–14 Baisakhi (Sikh)
13–16 Songkran (Thailand)
23 St. George's Day (England)
23 Çocuk Bayrami/Children's Day (Turkey)
25 Anzac Day (Australia and New Zealand)
MOVEABLE:
Passover (Jewish)

April/May

Mothers' Day (USA)
Eastern Orthodox Easter (Christian)

May

1 May Day (Northern Europe)
1 Labor Day (UK, Russia)
5 Kodomono-hi/Boys' Day (Japan)
MOVEABLE:
Cheung Cha Bun Festival (Hong Kong)
Fête des Mères (France)
Memorial Day (USA)
Pentecost (Christian)

May/June

Shavuot (Jewish)
Wesak (Buddhist/Sri Lanka)
Mother's Day (USA)

June

MOVEABLE:
Duan Yang/Dragon Boat Festival (China)
Fathers' Day (UK, USA)

July

4 Independence Day (USA)
13–16 Obon/Family Remembrance Day (Japan)
14 Bastille Day (France)

July/August

Asalha Perahara (Buddhist/Sri Lanka)
Palio (Siena, Italy)

August

1 African Emancipation Day (Jamaica)
MOVEABLE:
Edinburgh Arts Festival (Scotland)
Notting Hill Carnival (London, England)
Raksha Bandhan (Hindu)

August/ September

Feast of Hungry Ghosts (China)
Janamashtami/Krishna's Birthday (Hindu)

September

MOVEABLE:
Dassehra (Hindu)
Labor Day (USA, Canada)
Oktoberfest (Germany)
Rosh Hoshanah (Jewish)

September/ October

Yom Kippur (Jewish)
Sukkot (Jewish)
Trung Thu (Vietnam)

October

2 Gandhi Jayanti (India)
12 Columbus Day (USA)
12 Dia de la Raza (Colombia)
31 Halloween

Jack-o'-lantern

October/ November

Divali (Hindu)
Guru Nanak's Birthday (Sikh)

November

1 All Saints' Day (Christian)
1–2 Day of the Dead (Mexico)
2 All Souls' Day (Christian)
5 Guy Fawkes' Night (UK)
9 Anniversary of Fall of the Berlin Wall (Germany)
11 Veteran's Day (USA)
15 Shichi-go-san/Seven-three-five (Japan)
23 New Taste Festival/Labor Day (Japan)
30 St. Andrew's Day (Scotland)
MOVEABLE:
Thanksgiving Day (USA)
Remembrance Day (UK, Canada, NZ)

Christmas wreath and candle

December

6 St. Nicholas' Day (Christian)
13 St. Lucia's Day (Christian)
24 Christmas Eve (Christian)
25 Christmas Day (Christian)
26 Boxing Day/St. Stephen's Day (Christian)
31 New Year's Eve (Gregorian calendar)
31 Hogmanay (Scotland)
MOVEABLE:
Hanukkah (Jewish)

December/ January

Kwanzaa (USA)
Guru Gobind Singh's Birthday (Sikh)

National Days

January
26 Australia
26 India
31 Nauru

My relatives in India hold their national day on January 26.

February
4 Sri Lanka
6 New Zealand
7 Grenada
11 Japan
18 The Gambia
22 St Lucia
23 Brunei
23 Guyana

March
6 Ghana
12 Mauritius
21 Namibia
23 Pakistan
25 Greece
26 Bangladesh
31 Malta

One of our Japanese national days is on January 11.

April
1 Inuit Independence Day
18 Zimbabwe
27 Sierra Leone
27 South Africa
30 Netherlands

Bastille Day is a French holiday.

April/May
Israel

May
3 Poland
5 Netherlands
17 Norway
20 Cameroon

My Israeli relatives have their national day in April or May.

June
1 Samoa
2 Italy
4 Tonga
5 Denmark
6 Sweden
12 UK (Queen's official birthday)
12 Russia
18 Seychelles
25 Mozambique

Sweden's national day is on June 6.

July
1 Canada
4 Independence Day, USA
6 Malawi
7 Solomon Islands
9 Argentina
10 The Bahamas
12 Kiribati
14 Bastille Day, France
21 Belgium
26 Maldives
30 Vanuatu

July 4 is a holiday for all Americans.

August
1 Switzerland
6 Jamaica
6 Bolivia
9 Singapore
17 Indonesia
31 Malaysia
31 Trinidad & Tobago

September
6 Swaziland
7 Brazil
16 Papua New Guinea
16 Mexico
18 Chile
19 St Kitts & Nevis
21 Belize
23 Saudi Arabia
30 Botswana

October
1 Cyprus
1 Nigeria
1 Tuvalu
1 China
4 Lesotho
9 Uganda
10 Fiji Islands
12 Spain
24 Zambia
26 Austria
27 St Vincent & the Grenadines

In Saudi Arabia we honor our kingdom in September.

November
1 Antigua & Barbuda
3 Dominica
30 Barbados

December
6 Finland
9 Tanzania
12 Kenya

Saints' Days

My name day is on April 16, the Feast Day of St. Bernadette. There are too many Christian saints' days to list them all, but here are some.

January
3   Hilary of Poitiers
20   Sebastian
28   Thomas Aquinas

February
1   Brigid
2   Blessed Virgin Mary
9   Apollonia
12   Julian the Hospitaller
14   Valentine
25   Walburga

March
1   David of Wales
7   Perpetua
8   John of God
9   Frances of Rome
17   Patrick
19   Joseph
20   Cuthbert

April
16   Bernadette of Lourdes
23   George
25   Mark
29   Catherine of Siena

May
3   James
3   Philip
10   Antonius of Florence
12   Pancras
14   Matthias
27   Augustine of Canterbury
30   Joan of Arc

June
1   Justin
2   Elmo
3   Kevin
9   Columba
11   Barnabas
22   Thomas More
24   John the Baptist
29   Paul
29   Peter

July
1   Oliver Plunkett
2   Swithin
3   Thomas
4   Elizabeth of Portugal
11   Benedict
22   Mary Magdalene
23   Bridget of Sweden
25   Christopher
25   James the Great
26   Anne
29   Martha

August
10   Lawrence
11   Clare of Assisi
23   Rose of Lima
24   Bartholomew
27   Monica
28   Augustine of Hippo

September
1   Giles
2   Agricola of Avignon
3   Gregory the Great
17   Hildegard
17   Lambert of Maastricht
18   Joseph of Copertino
21   Matthew
22   Maurice
28   Wenceslas
29   Gabriel the Archangel
29   Michael the Archangel
29   Raphael the Archangel
30   Jerome

October
4   Francis of Assisi
6   Faith
18   Luke
28   Jude
28   Simon
31   Wolfgang

November
1   All Saints
11   Martin of Tours
15   Albert the Great
16   Margaret of Scotland
17   Gregory the Wonderworker
20   Edmund of East Anglia
22   Cecelia
23   Columban
23   Felicity
30   Andrew

December
4   Barbara
6   Nicholas of Myra
7   Ambrose
12   Our Lady of Guadalupe
13   Lucia
26   Stephen
27   John the Apostle
29   Thomas à Becket

Glossary

Abraham a Prophet important in Jewish and Christian faiths, called Ibrahim by Muslims

Advent the four weeks before Christmas when Christians prepare for the approaching Nativity

Allah the name of God among Arabs and Muslims

amulet jewelry worn as a good luck charm

ancestor a relative in the distant past from whom someone is descended

anniversary the celebration of an event that happened one year ago

bank holiday a public holiday in Britain when businesses close down

baptism the religious ceremony symbolizing admission to the Christian Church

Baptist a branch of the Christian Church that performs baptism by completely immersing a person in holy water

Bar Mitzvah religious initiation for 13-year-old Jewish boys

Bat Mitzvah religious initiation for 12-year-old Jewish girls

Brit Milah the circumcision ceremony for Jewish baby boys

carnival the time in February when people have fun just before Lent

ceremony a formal religious or public occasion

circumcision a surgical operation to cut off the foreskin of the penis; a Jewish and Muslim birth custom

confirmation a religious ritual accepting a baptized person as a member of the Christian Church

contract a legal, written, or spoken agreement between two people

Covenant the agreement made between God (Allah) and Abraham (Ibrahim)

custom the usual way of doing something

dowry the property or money brought by a bride to her husband

Durga one of the many names of the Hindu mother goddess, Devi

fiesta a holiday; a religious festival in Spanish-speaking countries

float a decorated cart used to carry people as part of a street parade

flotilla a small fleet of boats

font a stone receptacle in church that holds holy water for baptism

Gaia in Greek mythology, the goddess of the Earth. Gaia theorists believe that the Earth is a single organism that can regulate itself.

generation all the people born at one particular time

Gregorian calendar the solar calendar adopted in the 16th century by most of the world

haroset a mixture of apples, nuts, and spices eaten by Jews at Passover

henna a reddish-brown natural dye used to decorate a Hindu bride's hands and feet

horoscope the forecast of someone's future based on the positions of the stars and planets when the person was born

Id or Eid the Muslim word for a festival, for example Id-ul-Fitr

imam the Muslim leader of prayers in the mosque

independence for a country, this means self-rule, rather than government by another nation

Indra a Hindu god

initiation the ritual by which a person is accepted into a group

karah parshad a holy food shared by Sikhs, symbolizing unity

khalsa the community of initiated Sikhs, founded in 1699

kimono a long, loose Japanese robe tied at the waist with a sash

Lakshmi Hindu goddess of wealth and beauty; Vishnu's wife

lunar calendar a way of measuring time used by Hindus and Muslims. A lunar month lasts 29.5 days, the time the Moon takes to circle Earth

medieval in history, the period from about AD 400 to around AD 1400

memorial an object or custom in memory of a person or event

Muhammad the last prophet of Islam. He died in AD 632.

novice someone who is learning to be something, for example a monk

Olympic Games an Ancient Greek festival held at Olympia. Now a modern international sports' festival held every four years since 1896

Orthodox traditional; there are Orthodox Christians and Jews

pagan people with no distinct religion or culture

prophet someone who passes on messages from God

rabbi a Jewish religious leader

reincarnation the rebirth of a person's soul in a new body

resolution a good intention, often made to oneself on New Year's Day

ritual a particular series of actions, such as those in a religious ceremony

Roman Catholic a Christian who recognizes the Pope as head of the Church

Sabbath a day of rest and religious observance; Saturday for Jews and Sunday for Christians

sacrifice killing of an animal or, in ancient times, a person, as an offering to a god or goddess

samsara one of 13 ceremonies that all Hindus go through to mark events in their lives

seder the Jewish Passover meal

shofar religious object for Jews; a ram's horn blown at Yom Kippur

shrine a sacred place; a container holding sacred objects

symbol an object or action representing something else

tilak a holy mark on the forehead made with red paste; Hindus regard this mark as symbolic of success

tomb an underground vault for the burial of the dead

tradition a way of thinking or behaving handed down from generation to generation

wreath a ring of flowers or leaves placed on a grave or memorial

Photographic sources and copyrights
Hutchison Photo Library: pages 7 (Michael Macintyre), 13 (Juliet Highet), 37 bottom (Jeremy Horner), 57 top (Sarah Murray). **Christine Osborne Pictures:** pages 11 (C. Boulanger), 12, 20, 33 left, 43, 53 top (B. Hanson), 54 bottom. **Impact Photo Library:** pages 15 (Mohamed Ansar), 21 (Tadashi Kajiyama), 28 (Stephen Hird), 29 and back cover (Simon Shepheard), 37 top (Michael Good), 54–55 (Caroline Penn). **TRIP:** pages 16 (Christopher Rennie), 26 top (M. Feeney), 31 top (H. Rogers), 38 bottom (K. Cardwell), 41 (Eric Smith), 48–49 (Dinodia), 51 (M. Mclaren), 52 (M. Garrett), 55 bottom (S. Shapiro).

Corbis Images: pages 17 top (Penny Tweedie), 17 bottom (Bob Krist) 19 (K. M. Westermann), 24 (Lyn Hughes), 25 (Kelly-Mooney Photography) 26 bottom (Franz-Marc Frei), 31 bottom (Marc Garanger), 34 (Phil Schermeister), 35 top (Dean Conger), 39 (Robert Maass), 42 (Keren Su), 46 (Adam Wolfitt), 49 bottom (Owen Franken), 53 bottom (Ted Spiegal), 56 (Bob Krist). **Eye Ubiqitous:** pages 30 (Adina Tovy Amsel), 35 bottom (Gavin Wickham), 45 (John Dakers), 49 right (Hans Nelsäter). **Camera Press:** pages 44 (Kevin Unger), 57 bottom (Lourdes Grobet). **Topham/Image Works:** page 37 bottom.
Studio photography by Steve Gorton (© Transedition).

Index